Theseus
and the Minotaur

Laura North and Ross Collins

W
FRANKLIN WATTS
LONDON•SYDNEY

Chapter 1:
A Terrible Secret

Long ago, Prince Theseus lived with his father, King Aegeus, in Athens.

One day, Aegeus told his son a terrible secret.
"Every year we have to send seven girls
and seven boys to King Minos in Crete.
They are eaten by a terrible monster called
the Minotaur."
"Why, father?" asked Theseus.
"King Minos had a son," explained Aegeus.
"He was killed accidentally in Athens.

"Minos was so angry that he attacked us and forced us to make this sacrifice."

5

"Father, this cannot happen any longer!
I will go with them and kill the beast!"
promised Theseus.

Aegeus begged him to stay but Theseus
refused to listen.

"Son," said Aegeus. "Do one thing for me. Change the sail on your ship to white if you survive. If it is a black sail, then I will know you are dead."

"Of course, Father," said Theseus, though he was so busy getting ready he hardly heard what his father said.

Theseus arrived in Crete. There was a throne in front of them, with a small man sitting on top. "I am the mighty King Minos," he announced. "I am so happy that we have food for the Minotaur!" he laughed.

Minos sent the young men and women to
the labyrinth, a huge underground maze
where the Minotaur lived. Theseus did not
know how he would defeat the monster.
"What have I done?" he thought to himself.
"Have I brought death on myself and my
friends?"
The tall dark door to the labyrinth slowly
creaked open.

Chapter 2:
A Helping Hand

Just as Theseus was walking in despair
towards the door, a young woman crept
up to him.

"Wait," she whispered, "I'm Ariadne,
King Minos' daughter."

"Then curses on you!" said Theseus.
"Your father has condemned us all
to death."
"Listen to me!" said Ariadne, urgently.
"I can help you."

Ariadne passed Theseus a sword and a ball of thread. "The sword will help you kill the Minotaur. If you leave a trail of thread behind you, it will help you find your way out of the maze."

"But," asked Theseus, confused, "why would you help me?"

Ariadne blushed. The truth was that she had fallen in love with this brave, handsome stranger from Athens. "But I'm not going to admit that to Theseus!" she thought. She looked back at him. "Just accept my help. I do not want to see the blood shed of 14 innocent people. And, besides, I hate my father. "

"Thank you, with all my heart," said Theseus. "If I come out alive, I will marry you and take you away from this place." Ariadne and Theseus smiled at each other. He gripped her hand. "Now, I must go," said Theseus. He turned and walked down the stairs into the darkness below.

Chapter 3:
Into the Labryinth

"It's so dark in here," said Theseus. "I cannot even see my hand in front of my face."

He walked forward slowly. Gradually, his eyes got used to the darkness and, as he went on, there was a little light from a torch on the wall.

The roof of the maze became lower, and soon he had to get onto his knees. For hours and hours he crawled in the darkness. "I have never felt so alone," he said, as he thought about his father back in Athens so far away. But he never forgot to unwind the thread behind him.

Suddenly, in the darkness, he heard a loud noise. CRASH!

Theseus froze. Then there was silence.
In front of him, he saw a torch on the floor.
"It must have fallen from the wall,"
he thought, and sighed in relief.
He continued crawling
through the maze.

Suddenly he heard a mighty noise.
"GROWL!"
Where did it come from? His heart began
to beat faster, now that he was no longer
alone in the dark. He looked quickly
to the left, and then to the right.
He couldn't see anything.

He heard footsteps.

"Thump, thump, thump."

Each footstep got louder. In a flash, a huge monster appeared. It had the body of man and the head of a bull. It was the Minotaur!

Chapter 4:
A Terrible Monster

The beast flashed its sharp teeth and
lunged towards Theseus. It had
huge yellow horns and
blazing red eyes.

Theseus was fast. He dived away from the Minotaur and hid behind a pillar.

The Minotaur charged towards him, and in seconds, he was again face to face with the horrible creature.

"ROAAAR!"

The sound from the beast sent a shiver down Theseus' spine. The Minotaur was starving and ready to tear him to pieces. Sharp claws stretched out towards him. Theseus moved quickly, and pulled out the sword that Ariadne had given him.

The monster stared at him. Theseus plunged his sword into the chest of the Minotaur. The Minotaur dropped to the floor, writhing in pain. But in a few short seconds, the beast was dead.

Theseus was filled with relief.
It was a few minutes before he
realised what his victory meant.
"I have killed the beast,"
he said. "I have
rescued my friends.
And I have freed Athens!"

Theseus grabbed the thread and followed it back to the entrance, as fast as he could.

It was daylight outside. The crowd let out a cheer when they saw Theseus, alive and well. Theseus ran over to Ariadne.

Theseus, Ariadne and the Athenians sailed away from Crete towards Athens and their happy ending. Surely this is the end of the story? But wait. There is more to come.

Chapter 5:
Broken Promises

Theseus celebrated and drank. He congratulated himself on his victory, and on how clever he was to slay the beast.

They sailed for days and days.

"I am so happy," said Ariadne. "The Minotaur can do no more harm – and I am with you, Theseus."

Theseus smiled. But he was becoming less interested in the woman who had saved his life. "I'm a hero," he said. "I don't need anyone else taking the credit for my victory."

One night, they landed on a beautiful island.

"Let's sleep here tonight," said Theseus to Ariadne. She smiled at him as they sat on the sand beneath the full moon.

As Ariadne slept soundly, Theseus climbed aboard his ship, leaving her there alone.

Theseus, free of Ariadne, raced towards home. He celebrated more, and drank more. He forgot to do the one thing that he promised his father. He forgot to change his sail to white.

Aegeus was waiting in Athens, anxious about his son. When he saw Theseus' ship approach, his heart filled with hope.

Then he saw the sail was black.

"Theseus must be dead!" he cried. In his despair, he threw himself into the sea.

Theseus was heartbroken. He named
the sea the Aegean, so his father would
always be remembered.

About the story

Theseus was the mythical king of Athens – a Greek hero who is said to have travelled widely and fought many monsters, including a giant pig. This story of *Theseus and the Minotaur* is a Greek myth, which is told by the Roman poet Ovid in his book *Metamorphoses* and by the Greek scholar Plutarch in his biography *Lives*. There are more than 250 myths in Ovid's *Metamorphoses* and Plutarch's *Lives* includes biographies of famous Greek and Roman men. Both books were written in the first century CE, but the stories they tell are still very popular today.

Be in the story!

Imagine you are Ariadne. What might you be thinking when you wake up on the beach without Theseus?

Now imagine you are Theseus. You have just returned to Athens and you have killed the mighty Minotaur. But your father is also dead. Now you must tell the people what has happened.

First published in 2014 by
Franklin Watts
338 Euston Road
London
NW1 3BH

Franklin Watts Australia
Level 17/207 Kent Street
Sydney
NSW 2000

A CIP catalogue record for this book is available
from the British Library.

The artwork for this story first appeared in
Hopscotch Myths: Theseus and the Minotaur

ISBN 978 1 4451 3023 1 (hbk)
ISBN 978 1 4451 3027 9 (pbk)
ISBN 978 1 4451 3026 2 (library ebook)
ISBN 978 1 4451 3025 5 (ebook)

Series Editor: Jackie Hamley
Series Advisor: Catherine Glavina
Series Designer: Cathryn Gilbert

Printed in China

Franklin Watts is a divison of
Hachette Children's Books,
an Hachette UK company.
www.hachette.co.uk